Let's Talk About Finances

A Path to Financial Wellness for Social Work Students and Graduates

Dr. Veronica L. Hardy, LCSW

Copyright © 2022 Dr. Veronica L. Hardy, LCSW
Nelson-Hardy Learning Institute

All rights reserved.

ISBN: 9798792107281

Although the author has made every effort to ensure that the information and websites in this book were correct at press time, the author does not assume and hereby disclaims any liability to any party for any loss, damage, or disruption caused by errors or omissions, whether such errors or omissions result from negligence, accident, or any other cause.

This is a work of fiction. This book is not intended as a substitute for the advice of financial professionals or mental health providers. The reader should regularly consult a financial professional or mental health provider in matters relating to finances or mental health and particularly with respect to any symptoms that may require financial investment guidance, mental health diagnosis, or medical attention.

DEDICATION

To all those seeking financial freedom.

CONTENTS

1 My Story in a Nutshell — 3

2 The Why — 18

3 Explore Your Financial Story — 35

4 What's on Your Financial Resume? — 59

5 The Art of the Side Hustle — 78

6 Enhance Your Marketability — 88

7 Let's Make this Real — 101

   Creative Financial Practice Ideas — 114

   Sample Budget and Savings Plan Sheets — 117

   Resources — 123

   About the Author — 125

   Notes Pages — 129

1

MY STORY IN A NUTSHELL

Be intentional – create your financial wellness on purpose.

Dear social work students and graduates, let me let you in on a little secret – there is no secret to paying off debt. The facts are, to pay off debt you would need to decrease your spending and/or enhance your income, while making good financial decisions along the way that will benefit versus harm your credit. That is the trick! Financial wellness starts in the mind. However, financial wellness does not take place in isolation from other areas of your life. It is critical to consider the multiple systems influencing your financial decisions, beliefs, feelings, and practices with money, as well as your future intentions – in other words, what would you like to change or enhance about your financial habits? To be financially well, which systems would need to shift in your life? What types of financial "pivots" do you need to make? How can you be intentional and take action?

Small Steps, Major Progress

As social workers, you already know to break major goals into small, actionable tasks. This enables your financial goals to be manageable. Attempting to tackle an overall goal, such as paying off all student loan debt, can be overwhelming and lead to feelings of discouragement and stop you from moving forward. So, let's begin with small steps, the things that can start happening now to build your financial wellness. For example, this book will take you through that process. You will start by learning about finances (financial literacy), understanding your thoughts toward finances (financial self-awareness), exploring your current financial situation, and exploring ways to prepare to decrease debt, build savings, and develop other forms of income.

Be intentional about building financial wellness. Carve out 10 to 15 minutes a day to learn about finances. Be a student learning about finances daily such as reading an article, watching a video, talking to a financial counselor. Determine the specific subjects you would like to learn more about such as investing, loan payoff strategies, developing a budget, saving for education or vacation. Organize your learning tools such as notebooks, journals, folders, whatever works best for you. Build your knowledge so you can be strengthened and encouraged to keep traveling along your financial journey.

I have observed that the more I learn about finances, the more I want to know. I become aware of the types of questions to ask, where to locate resources, and what information is beneficial for my life and financial goals. I feel inspired and motivated to keep learning and to try out new ideas. Every day, you could make progress simply by being intentional about learning and carving out 10 to 15 minutes per day. Now that you have a daily learning plan, let's define financial wellness.

What is Financial Wellness?

Financial wellness is a state of mind and decision making that leads a person to feel a sense of comfort with their financial present and future; to have an awareness of skills necessary to maintain that financial comfort through monitoring their finances, avoiding excessive use of credit (e.g., loans, credit cards), abstaining from monetary waste, utilizing practices such as budgeting, contributing through practices such as donating, building financial literacy through education, maintaining awareness of beneficial resources (e.g., grants, scholarships), the ability to distinguish between what is essential and what is simply a want or desire, and investing wisely. Financial wellness is a continuous, intentional, and strategic practice that contributes to your physical, mental, and social wellbeing and enhances your unique quality of life. Yes, that is a long definition, but I wanted to make sure I captured the elements of financial wellness.

A Financial Wellness Workbook?

What problem was I trying to solve when I wrote this book? The intention of this book is to help provide insight to support you in gaining relief from financial stress. In addition, to enhance your financial literacy so you may advance in life according to your personal values and vision. You may have purchased this book because you have a need, want, or desire to be free from debt or to enhance your financial wellness. This book is a starting point for building a financial wellness mindset. Multiple other resources are noted throughout this writing for you to take the reins and continue your financial growth journey.

Not Just for Social Workers

I must stress; this book is not just for social workers!!! Yes, because I have social work and counseling degrees, there is language and examples relevant to those professions used throughout the book. However, the information may be helpful for anyone in any profession because finances are finances! Also, this book is not just for students. You may be a graduate but experiencing debt. This book is also for you!

Financial wellness is beneficial for everyone. No matter what degree program you are attending, what career you are in, or stage of education or life, explore what information may be applicable to your life. Feel welcome to navigate through these pages and apply the information that is best for you. Now that we have established the purpose behind this book, here is my story in a nutshell of putting several financial wellness skills into practice.

My Story

I enjoy working! There are several aspects I enjoy – creating, interacting with others, addressing challenges, and more. I began working when I was in high school at a place called Country Fair French Fries in the local mall. At the time, I was 15 and needed working papers since I was below the appropriate working age. The pay was $3.15 per hour. I enjoyed every moment of working in the mall, the local hangout spot for teens. Not to mention, we were directly next to the arcade. Exciting!

I held several more jobs during my teenage years. One of which was a co-op (cooperative education) job during high school. In other words, I attended classes during the morning, then in the afternoon I went to work in a human resource role at the cable company. This enhanced my education as I was learning how to make and manage money, building time management skills, and how to engage with others in the workplace.

During this time, my parents guided me in pursuing my very first investment, which was a certificate of deposit (CD). This was my first form of passive income, which gained interest while simply sitting at the credit union for a stipulated period. At that time, in the 1980s, the interest rates for CDs were great in my opinion. The CD and all the interest gained helped contribute to my undergraduate education.

Throughout my undergraduate years, I learned quite a bit about finances. After my first semester of having fun and noticing a not so pleasing grade on my transcript, I made an intentional decision that my parents were not paying for me to go to college to attain low grades. In my mind, that would be dishonoring them and wasting my family's finances. I made a shift! Classes were my priority and I had to make the necessary adjustments if I still wanted to have fun. What happened next? I developed a study strategy. As we know, you cannot add more hours to a day, but you can adjust the way the hours are used.

I decided to use my morning hours differently and started to get up around 5am, put on my desk lamp, took out my notes and books and started studying. I placed my information on index cards and as I walked across campus, I could use that time to study. These methods worked. At that time, there were no laptops, cell phones, or technology as we know it now. Eventually, my roommate started getting up at the same time while stretching and rubbing her eyes, but we did it. The outcome was higher grades, and I also received an unexpected scholarship every semester if my grades stayed high. Wow!

As far as income, I made the most of my summers and free time during the semesters by working at places including Arby's, Dorney Park, clothing stores, factories, and more. That was all in the early to mid-1990s. I had a mindset to contribute as much as I could to my education, honor my family's finances, and realize my degree was for more than just me ... it was also for my family and our future.

In reflecting on 1997-1999, I remember paying out of pocket for the Master of Social Work degree by working an overnight full-time job, part-time jobs, along with side hustles including selling items through consignment shops. Eventually, in 2002, I was intentional about becoming debt free because I planned to transition into self-employment. To do so, I worked full-time and part-time for at least a year to pay off any debt (e.g., car) before making the big transition and leaving what I perceived as my safety net of full-time employment and benefits. The process paid off, my business was successful, and I remained debt free while working between 15 to 20 hours per week.

In 2005, I decided to invest further in myself and career by pursuing a doctorate degree. It took me approximately a year to determine what type of degree would be in alignment with my life. However, the time to study available programs, learn about the value of the degree, ways it could be used, and exploring possible funding opportunities was worth it. While I previously attained a Master of Social Work degree, in 2006 I returned to school for a Doctorate in Counselor Education and Supervision.

During the process of seeking a doctoral program, I engaged with alumni from the program to gain their insights. I was also able to learn about funding options that I did not have to pay back, such as grants and scholarships. Since I was debt free at the time, I decided to use the university's payment plan option since the degree was my most significant bill (other than rental space for my business and health insurance). During my final year of the doctoral program, I was drawn to a desire to teach. This led me to apply to social work programs across the country. I said "yes" to two opportunities out in the western part of the United States, packed my bags, and moved. Certainly, the move across country was a significant expense.

After a couple of years living in my new location and the completion of my degree, I decided to be closer to family. This led to another trek across the country and selecting my first home. Luckily, President Obama was in office at the time and there were great options for first-time homebuyers such as no down payment. Fantastic!

Let's recap. By that time, I transitioned into self-employment, experienced two relocations in a short period of time, completed a doctorate degree, and secured my first home. In other words, I accumulated debt, all with a purpose – family and career. Paying off any remaining degree and relocation debt was a primary focus. I targeted those balances and, in 2010, they were paid off in approximately a year after I graduated and relocated. I then focused on the vehicle, which was paid off soon after. All that remained was the home mortgage and enjoying life.

Let's fast forward to 2021, where I am debt free once again! It did not take long considering my number of investments in education, housing, vehicles, and even the daily bills, much needed vacations, and certainly my church tithe – which always comes out of my paycheck first. I made decisions that were beneficial for my life, which included full-time employment, periodic contract work that was enjoyable and consistent with my career, and even fun side hustles in alignment with my creative side. I also made the decision to focus on what matters when it came to how I used my money and the ways I navigated my life overall.

A Little More about Me

Timing is critical! I temporarily abstained from fulfilling certain plans and intentions because I wanted to pay off my mortgage and be debt free. I was able to strategize and accomplish all this during two floods and even a pandemic. What a memorable experience to navigate career and finances during such a time. Now that I stacked my deck, doubled-up on work, and hustled so I could pay the house off, I can now begin the next phase of re-investing in myself.

Career-wise, I can begin working on making myself more marketable as I enter this next phase of life. I have been blessed to live almost a half-century. I realize it is okay or even necessary to make myself relevant for the current career landscape. I believe it is incredible for someone in their field to dive out and do something new rather than sit in regret wishing they had. I want to be one of those people to dive out!

At the time of this writing, I am a Professor of Social Work, career mentor, and author. I maintain a mentorship website to encourage and uplift fellow social workers at veronicahardy.com. I have a second website that I use to highlight my professional accomplishments at drveronicahardy.com. Further, I am a featured writer and YouTuber for The New Social Worker: The Social Work Careers Magazine founded by social work pioneer, Linda Grobman. In addition, I maintain a Facebook group for social workers, The Social Work Lounge.

What is next on my list? My vision includes writing, engaging in more public speaking opportunities, and providing counsel in diverse ways. This will also allow me the opportunity to do more activities that matter – such as enhancing my focus on child sex trafficking and confronting further social injustices including racial and ability inequities. That's my story in a nutshell. Now let's talk about first-generation college students.

A Message to First-Generation College Students

As a first-generation college grad, I have found that we are often defined from a deficiency perspective that overlooks strengths that we have been exposed to during our upbringing from parents, caregivers, or others in our environment. During your upbringing, what did you learn about academics, time management, and career within your household or from broader society? What you learned may not have been through conversation but through observation. What did you see, hear, or experience? Consider how those skills can translate into an academic environment or even career. Primarily, I want to send you the message that you are not deficient, inadequate, or an imposter in the academic world. Instead, you are brilliant, capable, and a person with purpose. Remember your identity!

Economic Inequality and Finances

As social workers, we are grounded in social justice efforts including economic justice. Economic inequalities have contributed to the financial vulnerabilities experienced by many. Although social workers, we are still impacted by several of the same experiences of those to whom we provide services. In other words, several fellow social workers have also experienced upbringing in financially vulnerable households, thus affecting other current day circumstances and money practices. This was an important factor for me to consider while developing this financial wellness tool.

Economic wellbeing includes access to healthy work environments and equal pay that helps provide for your basic needs across your lifespan. There are documents within the social work profession that address issues related to economic wellbeing, including your economic health as a social worker. Let's take a moment to dive into the literature. The American Academy of Social Work and Social Welfare (2016) developed a document titled, Progress and Plans for the Grand Challenges: An Impact Report at Year 5 of the 10-Year Initiative. Within this document, thirteen grand challenges are noted, two of which are: (1) Build Financial Capability and Assets for All, and (2) Reduce Extreme Economic Inequality. Furthermore, the National Association of Social Workers (NASW) provides the 2021 Blueprint of Federal Social Policy Priorities: Recommendations to the Biden-Harris Administration and Congress. In viewing this document, you will also recognize the inclusion of the two grand challenges noted above, as well as Supporting Our Essential Social Work Workforce.

Task: Conduct an internet search to locate the Grand Challenges and Blueprint documents mentioned above. In the space below, write what you have learned from reading these documents. How can the information in the documents be helpful as you build your financial wellness?

There is an awareness that multiple disparities exist due to factors including systemic oppression. As a result, there are various issues that impact a person's financial standing. For example, geographic location affects access to strong education systems, thus affecting job access and income opportunities, as well as access to adequate healthcare services (the primary reason people are in debt is due to healthcare reasons). Income is further affected by factors including the employer, funding sources, size of organization, and cost of living. These elements have a strong impact on economic wellbeing and financial wellness.

Trauma and Finances

For a lifestyle change, you must find out the root of why you are in debt. Why? Oftentimes, people may start new behaviors for the short term, but eventually motivation decreases, and they stop moving toward the goal. However, for the long game, you need to find out what is going on, and what led to the choices and behaviors that may have led to unhealthy financial decisions. For example, some people may overspend because they experienced extreme lack as a child or other early life experiences. There is an avoidance of the mental stuff in many financial writings. In my reading of financial literature, I have noticed there is limited discussion about the role of mindset, emotions, societal circumstances, or trauma in relation to finances.

Certainly, this book was not written as a form of counseling, and I recommend engaging in professional mental health services if experiencing persistent and overwhelming mental health difficulties with trauma-related issues. However, I want to make sure to acknowledge the relationship between trauma and finances. As I previously mentioned, there are multiple systems and types of inequalities that impact the way we navigate our finances. I often have had the opportunity to hear experiences related to finances as a trigger of trauma responses.

There are experiences of suffering, themes of lacking access to employment opportunities or health care services. There are experiences of lack of food, therefore keeping food products several years after the expiration date – just in case. There are experiences of being controlled by others through financial and economic abuse (e.g., intimate partner/domestic violence). In other words, restricting a person's choices and access to opportunities.

Further, trauma can be related to finances through various forms of abuse such as when parents or caregivers commit identity theft of their children. What does this mean? Is it possible? Yes, it is very possible and seen as a form of abuse and crime. Oftentimes, children will not tell because they do not want to get their loved ones in trouble. Many do not realize their credit has been misused by their parents until they apply for college loans. Financial trauma can also extend from poverty, the effects of natural disasters, and other systemic or unexpected circumstances, even for fellow social workers.

Overall, financial wellness is impacted by more than just a person's individual decision making, it is also affected by systemic factors. Therefore, as you navigate this book, your story and process will be different from mine. Each of us are unique, our situations vary, and our access to resources are impacted by broader systems. My hope is to promote economic wellbeing by creating awareness about resources available and generating a sense of empowerment through knowledge building. Even more so, you will see tasks throughout this book prompting you to proactively gain information and enhance your financial literacy.

Task: Let's take a moment to pause. I invite you to use the space below to describe the various systems (past and present) that may be impacting your financial decisions and circumstances. A system could be family, healthcare, racism, genderism, ableism, and more.

Finances and Self-Care

Over the years, I have been intentional about staying in alignment with what is important for me. For example, clutter is distracting for me, so I abstain from purchases that are not necessary. I enjoy donating and volunteering. I focus on healthy eating, cooking, and growing as much of my own food as possible. I stay consistent with exercise and, although I once had a fitness membership, I now workout at home and maintain equipment I can use at my leisure. Each of these decisions has been fulfilling and contributes to the enhancement of my life. It seems the older I get, I have been able to gain clarity about what is important, at least for my life. Maintaining financial wellness and freedom from debt are two of those important areas.

As a social worker, I realize how financial overwhelm contributes to varying levels of stress and anxiety, symptoms of burnout, and even high turnover rates in the workplace. We are often taught about self-care – however, there is little discussion about how financial wellness is a key self-care technique that is necessary for our wellbeing. The basic needs of social workers include developing a healthy relationship with finances, developing financial management skills, and integrating this with other systems in our lives.

Therefore, I developed this workbook to respond to this unique self-care need. When designing the workbook, I figured it could be a starting point for building financial wellness. I am certainly not a financial expert regarding investments, types of accounts, retirement, etc. I just have my own story and some tips that may be helpful for others. As a result, the objectives of this workbook include sharing my personal narratives, providing the basics of financial wellness, recognizing the long-term impact of student loans, and identifying skills for basic financial planning. In other words, my hope is that this workbook will get you started on the path to financial wellness, and that you will be strategic and take action to keep growing. This is just the beginning!

Let's Begin

Task: Well, those are my financial and career stories in a nutshell, future intentions, and purpose for writing this book. Now, let's begin focusing on yours with the following question: **How knowledgeable do you feel about financial management?**

1. Very knowledgeable

2. Moderately knowledgeable
3. A little knowledgeable
4. Not at all knowledgeable

Based on the answer you selected above, use the space below to describe what has positively or negatively affected your financial knowledge level.

Next, describe what you hope to learn about finances through this workbook. Also describe what you hope to learn about yourself and your financial habits.

What is your financial vision? What do you hope your finances will be like 5, 10, or 15 years from now?

It is time to write "why" you chose to purchase this book. Why are you seeking to enhance your financial wellness? It is important to know and understand your why and remember your reason. For example, do you want to break a legacy of financial struggle? Do you want to enhance your life? Do you want to pursue a lifelong goal and need the finances to do so? Whatever it is, write your "why" and periodically reflect on this as a source of motivation and encouragement to remain consistent in your financial wellness journey.

2
———

THE WHY

Intentional changes in your habits - can lead to major "wins" in your financial wellness.

Bank of America, one of the largest banking and financial institutions in the United States, conducts reports on spending habits across various populations. In 2020, Bank of America provided a document titled, Better Money Habits: Millennial Report Winter 2020. Certainly, many of you – including myself, are not labeled as millennials, but this information may still be helpful as you build your financial wellness mindset.

Side note … as social workers, we are also researchers. When reviewing documents using forms of research, always consider the sample size. The sample size for this study was quite small with 1,903 respondents ranging from 18-73 years of age, only a portion were millennials. Therefore, consider that as you view a few of the directly quoted findings below from the report:

- Despite financial progress, 51 percent of millennials feel behind in their overall financial situation and 33 percent believe their peers are better off financially. Seventy-three percent are not optimistic about their financial future.
- Seventy-six percent of millennials carry debt of some kind, with 16 percent owing $50,000 or more, excluding home loans. Of those with debt, 76 percent say they can't achieve their personal and financial goals because of it.
- Debt is a serious financial obstacle for millennials. More than three-quarters (76 percent) carry debt of some kind, including student loans and credit card debt.
- Still, 90 percent of millennials are willing to make sacrifices to achieve a financial goal, including cutting back on dining out (70 percent) and eliminating vacations (35 percent).

Just as we do in social work practice, Bank of America's intention in gathering this information is very consistent with a needs assessment. In other words, obtaining insights from the target population to identify and address gaps in services. As you view the information above, what are the needs? What are the challenges experienced by the target population (e.g., millennials)? What may be the impact on mental health and wellness? Even if you are not a millennial, are there ways you may be experiencing similar challenges?

Task: Conduct an internet search and locate the Better Money Habits: Millennial Report Winter 2020 as well as any reports from previous years. Below, describe your reactions to the information in the reports. Identify any new insights you may have gained from studying these reports.

Addressing Financial Wellness Gaps

There are multiple gaps this workbook is designed to address including the lack of exposure to finance-related topics during educational programs, the importance of developing debt payoff strategies, and practicing financial wellness as a form of psychosocial wellbeing. Let's begin by exploring social work and debt. The quote, "I believe that unmanageable debt, poor preparation in training for job negotiations, and low salaries in the social work profession make the social work profession untenable," is from an individual who participated in the National Association of Social Workers (NASW) Membership Workforce Survey 2007 report titled, In the Red: Social Workers and Educational Debt.

The intention of this study was to further explore the workforce stressors experienced by social workers, including educational debt and career pivot points. However, what is debt? Basically, when you owe someone or an entity money, this means you are in debt. You may be in debt to a credit card company, loan organization, or even a medical facility. There are many ways debt may be incurred. The goal is to pay your bills on time and pay more than the minimum payment, when possible. This helps your credit history (the process that tracks your debt and credit patterns – more about this later in the book).

Certainly, further studies have taken place since 2007 (visit Workforce Studies at www.socialworkers.org), but the ongoing themes across studies are debt and income challenges. Thus, contributing to a further discussion about money management and financial wellness amongst social work students and professionals. The Type of Educational Debt chart in the NASW Membership Workforce Survey (3,653 survey participants) shows 95% of participants identified student loan debt, 31% were primarily experiencing credit card debt, and 12% stipulated their debt as "other."

According to the Type of Educational Debt information, student loan debt is a primary source of debt for social workers. A survey participant quote states, "Try to find a way to pay for school other than loans." However, an additional thought is, what types of educational choices are contributing to such high student loan debt? For example, what is the role of the lack of data collection about education-related expenses or even brand shopping as some of the debt-causing factors?

Overall, debt is harmful when you do not have enough money to pay it back. Do you currently have debt, such as a credit card, that you cannot pay back? Have you ever skipped payments? Have you ever paid below the minimum amount due? If so, it is time to strategize how to avoid getting into debt OR how to get out of debt. Before doing so, let's talk about several more reasons social workers may be experiencing debt.

Limited Planning

Limited planning for educational pursuits contributes to the reasons social workers may be in debt. When pursuing education, it is critical to consider multiple factors including the cost, your income, geographic location, household expenses, gas prices, cost of internet, childcare, etc. Here, let's talk about the cost and how to obtain that information.

Did you know that each college or university may have a net price calculator on its website? According to the U.S. Department of Education, these calculators allow prospective students the opportunity to type in their information, including:

- o Your age
- o Whether or not you are applying for financial aid
- o Whether you qualify for in-state or out-of-state tuition

The calculator then outputs information previous students in your similar situation paid for estimated expenses including tuition and fees, room and board, books and supplies, and other personal expenses. This is very helpful for planning purposes when selecting a degree program and organizing your finances. However, what the calculator outputs is not the only consideration. What about your personal financial habits?

You know your habits and interests better than anyone. How often do you give attention to and document your financial habits? Examine your habits and take time to factor in entertainment, clothing, meals during outings, existing debt, etc. Considering these additional expenses will provide you with a broader picture of your expenses when attending college.

Gaining information from the net price calculator is critical for decision making and planning. However, this is not the only consideration. Your income also matters. We will talk more about income a little later. To learn more about the net price calculator, why higher education costs are increasing, and to access tools including the College Financing Plan, College Affordability and Transparency List, College Scorecard, and College Navigator, complete the task below.

Task: Conduct an internet search for the U.S. Department of Education, College Affordability and Transparency Center. Navigate the various tabs and describe below what you have learned.

Task: Visit a college or university website and search for "Net Price Calculator." Then, complete the requested information. Describe your findings in the space below.

Brand Shopping

Another factor that may contribute to social workers being in debt is brand shopping. Are you a brand shopper? If so, this is a brief note about brand shopping and the impact on financial wellness. A November 2021 article by The Wall Street Journal was posted online titled, USC Pushed a $115,000 Online Degree. Graduates Got Low Salaries, Huge Debts. The main theme was how a prominent non-profit university used a for-profit organization to recruit students to its social work program.

The article further highlights how various historically, socially, and economically oppressed populations were targeted through recruitment methods identified as aggressive. The result? Significant debt for multiple students. Reportedly, the article mentions unethical recruitment methods were implemented. In addition to the unethical recruitment methods, there is a further component to consider … brand shopping. Students need to be aware of unethical recruitment tactics, hidden costs due to for-profit organization use, as well as falling subject to brand shopping.

According to the article, a reason many students may have been drawn to that particular social work program was due to the "name" of the university. In other words, rather than learning about the quality and accessibility of the program, in addition to assessing one's own income, the choice may have been made based on the name of the university. Brand shopping.

Beware, brand shopping can be harmful to your financial health. Education is a form of investment into self, career, and family. Prior to selecting a university, ensure that choosing an educational institution for such an important investment will yield proper returns. In other words, will you profit from that investment in the long run? Or will you experience a loss from that investment – like that highlighted in

The Wall Street Journal article? Overall, be strategic about how you use your money and the institutions you choose.

Task: Conduct an internet search to learn more about Return on Investment (ROI). After conducting your search, use the space below to write what you have learned.

How can you apply what you have learned about ROI to your own financial decision making?

What are the reasons you think certain social work students and graduates are experiencing unmanageable debt?

Below, describe any debt avoidance or debt management strategies you currently use.

Professional Boundaries

Another factor that may contribute to social worker debt is lack of professional boundaries. As social workers, we are often obliged to give our time away, give our skills away, and give our talents away. This is certainly okay to do, however, at what level are you doing this? What type of impact is this having on your personal finances through costs such as travel, meals, or even the purchasing of office products to complete tasks? Is this contributing to symptoms of burnout due to overscheduling yourself and stretching yourself too thin? Does it affect the amount of valuable time you can spend with loved ones (let's not take time with loved ones for granted)? It is always important to consider what is realistic, in alignment with your life, and what will not exhaust your finances or push you to contribute beyond your means.

I have learned it is important to have boundaries within my career. I have learned the importance of setting limits and avoiding what I refer to as the "guilt syndrome." In other words, feeling the pressure that you "should" be able to volunteer without limits, however feeling guilty when you are not able to do so. Throw off the guilt syndrome, do the best you can within your means, and make sure you have time for you and those you love. These decisions are important for your financial, emotional, mental, spiritual, relationship, and physical health. Keep volunteering within a reasonable perspective and strategically plan your volunteer efforts. Then, you will have energy and time within your schedule to monetize your skills and pursue exciting new endeavors.

Fees After the Degree You May "Not Be" Taught About

Something that often receives little discussion during formal education is how to plan for the fees after the degree. What do I mean by this? Although not required, you may have an interest in pursuing certifications, licensure, attend conferences or trainings, or join professional organizations after attaining your degree that may contribute to debt. There are fees attached to each of these growth opportunities, including supervision fees for licensure. In addition, there may be dues, renewal, or recertification fees. To attend conferences, there may be travel, lodging, and meals to consider. My main point is, start researching your interests as soon as you can so you can begin budgeting for them. Here are some examples:

1. National Association of Social Workers $236 (membership types and costs vary)
2. Association of Social Work Boards Clinical Licensing Exam $260 (based on year 2021)
3. Conference rates can have a broad range, such as up to $700
4. Certifications and training prices range based on the type of certification and specific organization providing the training

Task: Conduct an internet search for certain of your areas of interest. For example, are you interested in clinical social work licensure? Visit your state social work board website to learn about the application fee and fees to maintain your license. Then visit the Association of Social Work Boards site to learn more about the clinical social work exam cost. Look up social work-related conferences taking place this year and the registration fees. Conduct a search for trainings or certifications you may be interested in. This task is designed to help you begin learning about what additional growth opportunities may cost.

Next, describe your findings. What growth opportunities did you search for? What were the fees? How might this affect your savings goals? Have you considered developing savings specifically for professional growth and development opportunities?

Your Income Matters

There are multiple factors that may impact your financial standing including brand shopping, spending beyond your means, limited planning, lack of boundaries, geographic location, and even economic inequality issues. Another factor is your actual income. According to the U.S. Bureau of Labor Statistics Occupational Outlook Handbook (2020), the reported median pay for social workers is $51,760 per year. Please note, the median is only one type of average (e.g., mean, median, and mode). This means 50% of the salaries fell below $51,760 and the other 50% fell above. This is quite a broad range as many social workers may make over $85,000 and several may make less than $33,000. This helps to enhance your awareness of the type of salary you can earn and what to negotiate when applying for jobs. However, this data does not seem to capture the wide diversity of environments in which social workers are employed. In other words, the data seems primarily based on what are labeled as traditional social work roles.

Task: Conduct an internet search to locate the U.S. Bureau of Labor Statistics Occupational Outlook Handbook information for social workers. Navigate the various tabs such as work environment, pay, job outlook, and state and area data. After reviewing the information, describe below how this information affects your financial planning. What type of information about the social work profession is "missing" from this website? Write your observations.

What are your salary intentions as a social worker?

30

What type of work environment would you prefer? How do you want to feel (e.g., energized, valued, overwhelmed, drained) in that work environment?

Task: Let's take a moment to explore some of your feelings around money. How do you "feel" when you spend money on: clothes, hygiene products, food, education, savings, fun stuff, donations, debt – interest payments, or bills? Use the space below to note your feelings for each of the items listed.

Next, reflect on what you have written above. What do you notice about the feelings? Are there some things you have strong feelings about? Are there some things that do not affect your feelings at all? Please write your thoughts.

The Way You Use Money

Remember, your income affects several of your life decisions and I have shared multiple factors that may affect your financial standing. Another factor is how you use money. Have you ever considered "why" you make certain purchases? Have you ever asked yourself the following questions prior to a purchase?

1. Do I really want to commit my money to this?
2. Is there another reason I want to buy this, such as my feelings are hurt, and I think this will help me to feel better?
3. Will spending money on this item keep me from fulfilling my budget?
4. Do I really need this item?

Guess what? You can choose something different. You can make new choices. Choices that are financially and emotionally healthy. One way to start doing this slowly is through a financial fast. You can start with a short one, such as a week, or a longer one, such as a month. Determine what might be comfortable for you. What would a financial fast consist of?

Let's Go on a Financial Fast – Challenge!

A financial fast would be an opportunity to intentionally use your money differently. Starting small can lead to big changes. A fast is a way of starting small so you can learn new spending behaviors and examine your thoughts and emotions toward money. For example, during the next seven days abstain from spending money, except for necessities such as bills, transportation necessary for work, school, or appointments; products needed to care for family members, medical necessities, etc.

At the end of your fasting period, take time to reflect and respond to the following questions:

1. What did you learn about your mentality toward finances?
2. What specific emotions did you experience? Do you know what triggered those emotions?
3. What did you learn about your spending habits?
4. What habits would you like to change?
5. What habits would you like to strengthen and build upon?
6. What new habits would you like to develop that will support you in building financial wellness?

Remember, intentional changes in your habits can lead to major enhancements in your financial wellness! Use the following space to record your thoughts.

Wow, you have done quite a bit already in navigating this book! For example, you have begun to assess your financial knowledge, explored systems that impact your life, visited websites, gained an understanding about the "why," and engaged in a financial fast! Keep up the great work! Now, let's go deeper into exploring your personal financial story, also known as a financial narrative.

3

EXPLORE YOUR FINANCIAL STORY

Recognize the root – then take action to create the changes you want to see.

As social workers, we have learned that narrative theory can help guide the exploration of one's story. Through the exploration of story, strategic and intentional change can come. Writing, verbalizing, and determining creative ways to express your narrative, the chapters, and themes can help to illuminate your knowledge about, and awareness of self. In doing so, you may come to realizations of themes you would like to "break away" from and "new chapters" you would like to write. You can explore narratives throughout multiple areas of your life ... including finances.

This financial assessment tool is designed to explore your relationship with finances, and to result in the initial development of your financial narrative – your unique story. Finances, and how we manage them, affect the types of decisions we can make, opportunities we can engage in, and even our self-perception. Finances may also be perceived as a form of self-expression through what we buy, the ways we give, and how we plan our future.

What types of financial choices have you been making? Have these choices been healthy? Unhealthy? Have they contributed to your life or detracted from your life? Have you prepared for the unexpected to the best of your ability? What themes have you noticed "replaying" in your financial story? What new chapters would you like to create? Let's take some time to explore your relationship with finances, the impact on your identity, and the pages of your financial story.

A Glimpse into My Financial Narrative

My financial narrative begins with my parents and the observations I had of them during my childhood. One of my earliest memories is how my mother used to do the grocery shopping for the family. I remember when she came home, the receipt seemed as if it was long as my forearm. At the time, my forearm was short since I was a child, but it looked like a grand list of things to me. She would place that receipt on a top shelf in the kitchen area of the house. Little did I realize, as a young couple with several mouths to feed, they had a system in place. Practices that seemed so simple were strong and necessary for this family.

Later, my dad would collect all the receipts that had been placed on the shelf and take them up to his desk. Once a month he would sit at that desk, put his desk lamp on, pull out a college ruled notebook, and start writing. I now realize he was recording the information from each receipt into that notebook. Then he would put all the receipts away.

With a family of six, it was important to organize the finances. To even highlight further, as an African American family, who had roots as farmers in the south, and engaged in the migration to a northern state, it was critical for their success and wellbeing to take control of their finances and engage in decision making that would be a strong foundation for their children to build upon. Not to mention, the forms of racism – oppression – experienced by this young family – my family - as part of the northern experience.

I'm thankful my parents provided me with this example of navigating the world and managing finances. I allowed these themes to continue throughout my life. I am happy I had the opportunity to observe my parents as a child, although not realizing that I was learning from them daily or how it would affect the way I navigated finances in my adult life. The modeling they presented to me about coordinating finances, how to communicate about finances, ways to document and notice where the money was going, and how the money was being used, had a significant impact on my life. An impact that still lives in me today. Money is a tool. It is important how we use it.

Writing Your Financial Narrative

On the next several pages you will notice personal questions related to your relationship with finances. Take your time in responding. You may need to take breaks and come back at a later point. You may need to ask others, who know you well, about the ways you engage your finances. Overall, this assessment is unique and personal to you. Take your time to capture your story, which will enable you to create and embrace a strong financial vision for your future. **Let's begin writing your financial narrative by developing responses to the following questions.**

First, how would you describe your relationship with finances? What influenced that relationship or understanding of finances?

Reflecting on your childhood, what observations do you remember about finances?

Were there any experiences of hurt or struggle related to finances during your childhood?

How has your spirituality, if any, affected your relationship with finances?

In what ways, if any, have social and economic injustices affected your relationship with finances?

In what ways, if any, does finances affect your self-perception?

In what ways, if any, does finances affect your personal relationships?

In what ways, if any, do you support others through your finances?

If you were to describe how you use your finances, what would you say?

In what ways, if any, do you donate money or items?

Reflecting on your experiences with finances, what have been your successes? Challenges? Disappointments?

Prior to pursuing higher education (college/university), did you plan how your finances would be used to attain this goal? Did you identify strategies to pay off loans as soon as possible?

Have you ever been drawn to spend money on something due to marketing strategies leading you to believe that you "must" have the product? For example, skincare, clothing items, vehicles, etc. Describe what draws you to these products.

How do you currently organize and track your finances?

What have been your greatest investments?

What tools or supports do you need to be financially empowered?

What steps can you take to build your financial literacy?

Next, look over everything you have written in response to the questions above and underline the themes. In other words, are there words, phrases, or experiences that keep repeating themselves throughout your responses or that cause a certain type of emotional reaction in you? Underline those themes.

Although I only wrote a glimpse into my financial story, here are a few of my themes:
1. Observations.
2. Parents.
3. Receipts.
4. System.
5. Notebook.
6. Family.
7. Navigating the world.
8. Communicating.

What are my reactions to these themes? I see several commonalities between how I have navigated my financial life and what I was exposed to during my early life stages. I unknowingly observed my parents' processes of managing finances. They never seemed stressed to me, but I realize that would only have been something they would have shown or discussed between each other, not in front of their children. They also lived within their means as we were always taken care of as children. Our residence was not cluttered with stuff. If we were ever in lack, I didn't know it. I also realized it was important to track how I used my money because it affects how I can navigate the world, interact with others, and even the types of environments I can step into. There are documents to help with this such as receipts. I have learned it is important to communicate with my partner or whoever I may be sharing a residence with about finances.

As I write my reactions to these themes, a word that comes to mind is "control." It is freeing to have a sense of empowerment and that the decisions I make contribute to this. Certainly, I have experienced times of financial stress when attending college, even when I was doing everything according to my idea of "right." But, at the same time, I was able to plan and take action to help reduce that stress through communicating and taking action. For example, contacting my landlord and requesting an extension on my rent for a week, asking my boss at a part-time job for more hours to enhance my income, or selling more items I no longer needed at consignment shops.

Reflect on your own themes and write your reaction to each one. What is that theme saying to you? What emotions arise as you reflect on those themes?

Identify whether each theme is a strength or foundation you can build upon or is it a challenge you would like to confront and overcome (e.g., a theme of money equals struggle)?

As you reflect on each theme, determine if they are being "replayed" in your adult life. Which themes would you like to change? Which themes would you like to keep?

Confront Your Loans

As you write your financial narrative and become empowered to manage your finances, it is important to evaluate your current circumstances. One of those circumstances may be student loans. The following quote is from the NASW Issue: Support Loan Forgiveness for Social Work Students and Graduates 2015, which states,

> "I currently hold an MSW degree. I have an outstanding student loan balance of over $150,000 for both undergraduate and graduate school. Unfortunately, a large chunk of that is in private loans through Sallie Mae and therefore I am not eligible for any kind of relief. I am currently employed full time making between

$40,000 and $50,000 a year. My current student loan payments (both federal and private) have me living at home with my father (I am 33) due to my inability to afford housing. I am unable to get any sort of credit extended to me because of my student loans. I am drowning in debt, literally, and will be unable to pull myself out in the foreseeable future."

The above quote shares the experience of many social workers pertaining to debt. To avoid increased debt, it will be important to manage your student loans. Being intentional about managing your student loans is a great way to improve your finances. On the next pages, take a few moments to determine the long-term impact of student loans on your finances through engaging in the Caleb Doe loan repayment exercise.

Scenario: Caleb Doe will be graduating with $30,000 in loan debt principal (the amount borrowed) for the undergraduate and graduate social work degrees combined. The interest rate on these educational loans is 5% (.05). Caleb plans to pay off the debt in 10 years. If Caleb does so, how much interest would have been paid during this time?

Directions: To answer the above question, conduct an internet search and access a loan repayment calculator such as on the finaid.org, bankrate.com, or your banking institution website and type in the following information:

- The loan amount (principal)
- The interest rate (%)
- The loan term in years
- The minimum payment (for this example you can use $0)
- Click calculate

Next, answer the following questions:

- What would Caleb's monthly loan payment be?
- What would Caleb's total amount of interest paid be in 10 years?
- By the end of 10 years, how much would Caleb have paid for the loan principal and interest?

Your Turn: Enhancing your knowledge about your loan trajectory is critical toward financial planning and wellness. This information will help you to strategize your next financial steps for paying loan debt. Now, it is your turn to give this a try with your own student loans, if any. Plug your information into a loan repayment calculator and determine:

- What would your monthly payment be?
- What would be your total amount of interest paid?
- By the end of your loan term, how much will you have paid in principal and interest?

Next, consider the following questions:

With this knowledge, are there any ways you would like to use your money differently?

In what ways can you be intentional in planning to pay off your student loan(s)?

If you did not have to pay that total amount of interest (e.g., if you paid off your loan early), what could you envision yourself using that money for?

Build a Growth Mindset

What is a growth mindset? A growth mindset means you seek to expand your knowledge, skills, and abilities by stepping out of your comfort zone. A comfort zone is a place of familiarity that you believe keeps you safe. On the contrary, a comfort zone can be a barrier to growth and progress. With a growth mindset, you seek to grow and stay open to healthy risks that can help move you toward your vision and intentions. Even more so, it is important to identify the barriers that hinder you and confront them by taking action. Don't just "think" about financial wellness, do it.

To build a growth mindset includes confronting negative thinking about your skills and abilities pertaining to finances. Certainly self-doubt, feeling like you don't deserve financial wellness, or comparing yourself to others who are already in a financially healthy place may lead you to devalue your skills and self-worth. In this case I pose the questions: What is underlying the feelings of self-doubt? What triggers thoughts of self-doubt? What leads you to compare yourself to others? What are the effects? I invite you to write your responses to these questions, if applicable.

I have had the opportunity to write several articles published in The New Social Worker: The Social Work Careers Magazine focusing on confidence, turning negative self-talk into empowerment-based talk, and even mental decluttering. Take a moment to stop by The New Social Worker website at socialworker.com and read a few of these articles. After doing so, share your thoughts in reaction to the material and how it relates to a growth mindset.

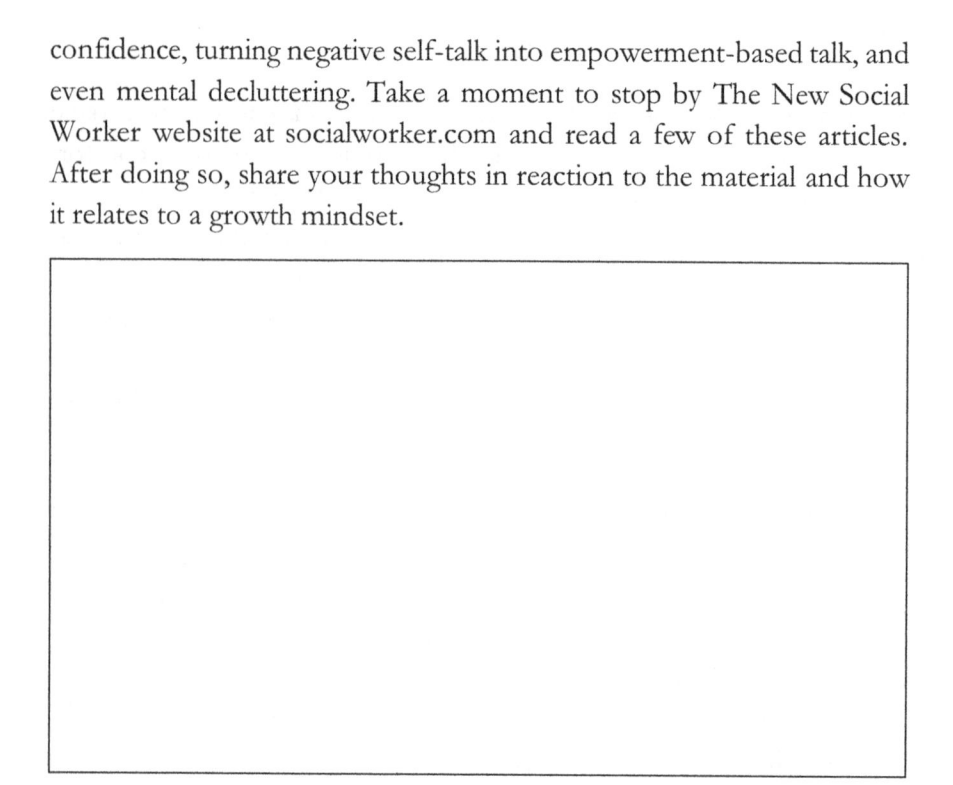

Now, let's look to the future. Insoo Kim Berg, a fellow social worker, co-developed solution-focused therapy (SFT). The intention behind this method was to build future-oriented goals (a growth mindset) that move us away from the challenges of the past and toward creating a new vision for the future. This is a creative way to shift our focus and motivate personal change. Consider how this could be applied to your financial wellness intentions. Solution-focused therapy uses many techniques, including the miracle question.

The miracle question can be quite helpful in creating a financial vision and gaining clarity about steps to achieve it. For example, if you were to wake up tomorrow and suddenly all your debt had been paid off, how would you feel? What emotions would you experience?

In what ways would your life be different?

In what ways would you use your money differently from that moment forward?

What would your future look like if you developed money habits that promoted financial wellness?

Overall, imagine what you want in life. Keep your responses to the above questions in mind. Now think about what you can start doing "today" to make all that happen. In other words, how you will take action. Several of your solutions lie in your answers to the above questions. The things you would do differently are the things you could begin doing now. What habits do you need to break? What is keeping you stuck in unhealthy financial patterns? What is one thing you can begin doing differently? Identify the thoughts and barriers that have kept you from moving forward, identify at least one new behavior or habit that could be implemented, then put it into action.

Why wait? Take a risk, enter a growth mindset, choose to use your money differently and consider what steps you will take to pay off your loans. Begin to create the future you envision. It is time to start writing the next chapter in your financial narrative. A new chapter that reflects goals toward financial freedom and resolution of debt. Keep reading for more insight into paying off debt and improving your finances.

The Answers

By the way, you may be wondering if you got the answers to the Caleb Doe Scenario questions correct. If so, the answers are below:

1. What would Caleb's monthly loan payment be?

   $318.20

2. What would Caleb's total amount of interest paid be in 10 years?

   $8,183.46

3. By the end of 10 years, how much would Caleb have paid for the loan principal and interest?

   $38,183.46

4

WHAT'S ON YOUR FINANCIAL RESUME?

Debt is a contract – fulfill your part of the deal so you can move to your next level.

Let's take some time to talk about credit and debt and gain a deeper understanding about your finances. Debt certainly plays a significant role when it comes to your financial health. Debt is a type of contract that you have made with an entity to use their money to pay for something. There is a condition in the contract that you will pay the money back, most times with interest, and according to a specific pay schedule. In other words, you signed a contract and must fulfill your part of the deal.

It is important that you find ways to fulfill your part of the deal because it can impact your access to credit or other financial contracts you may have access to in the future. In other words, it can impact your credit history and what others see about your financial habits. Your credit history is detailed through a credit report, which I refer to as a financial resume. This financial resume may be someone's (e.g., lender, realty agency, car salesperson) first impression of you, make it a good one!

Think forward to the future when you may want to borrow money to purchase a vehicle, buy a house, pay for more education, or even pay for unexpected medical expenses. the contractor (or lender) would want to see your financial resume (credit report) before allowing you access to funds (allowing you to borrow money). That person will want to see how much you already owe other lenders in comparison to what you make (your income). This is referred to as your debt-to-income ratio. You always want what you owe to be less than what you earn, or at least manageable.

What is a Credit Score?

They will also look at your credit score, more commonly referred to as the FICO (Fair Isaac Corporation) score. Here is an analogy to help understand the FICO score. The credit score is like a grade point average (GPA) for your education, which shows your average performance in courses. In other words, how well you did. Your GPA affects your academic choices and what type of program you can get into. The lower your GPA, the lesser your options may be. The higher the GPA, the greater your options.

A GPA is often interpreted as a person's commitment to their academic program, dedication to studying, and accomplishing the necessary tasks to attain the degree. The idea of a FICO score is quite similar. The higher your credit score, the more loan or credit options you may have and even lower interest rates. A high score may show that you have been credible with your finances, paid people back according to the contract, and were very consistent and timely with your payments. It may further convince lenders that you maintained consistent sources of income so you could pay back what you owed.

On the other hand, a low credit score may be interpreted as not being consistent, not making healthy financial decisions, meaning you would not be able to or would not be consistent in paying this new lender back. The lender may doubt if you can pay your bills on time and deny lending you money. A lower credit score could also result in paying higher interest rates. Remember the Caleb Doe scenario? You now know the importance and impact of an interest rate. You want it to be as low as possible. A low credit score can equal a high interest rate. Yikes!

While the academic programs you attend document a GPA (e.g., high school, college), there are also entities that document and make your FICO score available. Those entities are referred to as credit reporting agencies. Generally, a lender would contact those entities to gain information about your credit history and FICO score prior to determining if they will lend you money. There are three well-known credit reporting agencies (also referred to as credit bureaus) that document and maintain your credit reports and scores – TransUnion, Equifax, and Experian.

Review Your Credit Report

Did you know you can obtain a free copy of your credit report each year? This helps you to review the document, correct any errors, and keep track of your credit history. You may obtain a copy of your free annual credit report at the website annualcreditreport.com or by calling 1-877-322-8228. However, let's engage a few tasks to learn more about your credit report and why your credit history is important. **Tip:** It would be great to view copies of your credit report from each credit reporting agency since they each keep a file about your credit history.

Task: Conduct an internet search to locate the consumer.gov website. Navigate the tabs labeled as: What It Is, What to Know, and What to Do. Then, describe your learning.

Next, conduct an internet search for the website www.consumer.ftc.gov/articles/free-credit-reports. Navigate the information provided and describe what you have learned about avoiding credit report scams.

What information have you found about an exceptional, very good, good, fair, or poor credit score? Where do you fall within the range?

Be Intentional about Your Payoff Strategies

Now that you have learned the importance of your credit history as well as the value of that debt-to-income ratio, let's talk about strategies to help pay off debt. There are multiple strategies, however the strategies discussed below include: negotiating a lower interest rate, consolidating, loan forgiveness programs, snowball strategy, avalanche strategy, and budgeting. Remember, you can combine multiple approaches to maximize your success in paying off debt.

Build an emergency fund. Imagine this! You experience a medical emergency, the car breaks down and needs to get fixed right away because it is your only form of transportation, the refrigerator goes out and all your family's food will spoil, a natural disaster occurs, or you experience job loss. How would this affect you financially? Would you have enough money to pay for these unexpected circumstances? Would you have enough money saved to pay bills until you attain another job?

Before we get to strategies to pay off your student loan debt, let's talk about building an emergency fund. You may have heard about the importance of having what is referred to as a cushion, emergency fund, or savings available just in case unexpected situations happen. A rule of thumb, or recommended amount of savings for emergencies, is six months' worth of savings that would cover your bills. In other words, total what you usually spend per month on necessities, then save six months' worth (e.g., six months' worth of car payments, food bill).

However, it may be challenging to immediately save six months, so here are a few strategies – select a certain amount to place in an interest gaining savings account from each paycheck such as 2%, 5%, or 10%. – over time you could increase the amount. Another tip is to place any bonuses you receive from the workplace into savings. Determine ways you may gain income on the side (side hustle) with the intention of placing that income into savings. You could cut down on any unnecessary spending and place that money into the emergency fund. For example, review your subscriptions and memberships to determine what you could let go of or no longer use. Overall, set a clear savings goal that you can work toward. The development of a budget is discussed later in this chapter and can help you determine how much you will need for your emergency fund. There are also example savings goal sheets at the end of this book that may be helpful.

Is applying for loan forgiveness an option? What is this? This refers to programs that offer loan "forgiveness" for student loans only **IF** certain requirements are fulfilled. For example, the Public Service Loan Forgiveness program offers forgiveness to people who have worked for a government or nonprofit entity for 10 years. However, there is much competition for these, it may be challenging to attain … but worth it to apply. Be careful about early payments, deferred loans, or loans in forbearance as those payments may not count toward the loan forgiveness process. Please contact the student loan forgiveness program directly with questions.

Task: Conduct an internet search for the U.S. Department of Education and student loan forgiveness at www2.ed.gov/fund/grants-college.html.

Navigate to Public Service Loan Forgiveness. Study all the information about qualifications to apply, qualifying employers, qualifying payments, and more. After studying this information, describe your learning about the Public Service Loan Forgiveness program below.

Next, discuss whether you plan to apply for the program. Why or why not?

Task: To learn more about the Public Service Loan Forgiveness option, visit a copy of the application to learn what type of information is needed. To access a copy of the application, conduct an internet search

65

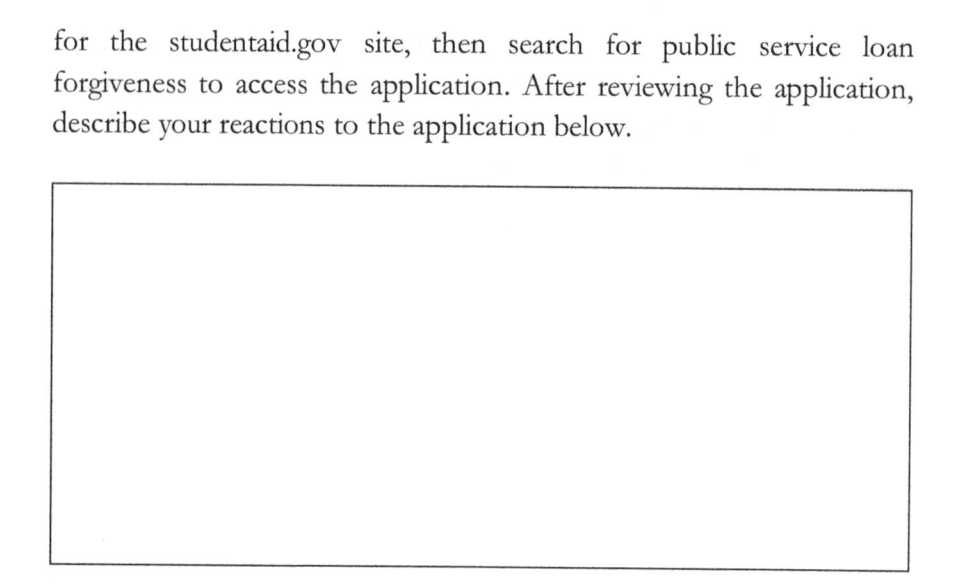

for the studentaid.gov site, then search for public service loan forgiveness to access the application. After reviewing the application, describe your reactions to the application below.

Is it possible to negotiate a lower interest rate? Remember, the higher your interest rate on a loan, the more you will have to pay in interest. Why not give negotiating a lower rate a try? Even lowering the rate by 1% can save you a lot of money. Revisit the loan repayment calculator you used earlier for the loan repayment exercise. Use the same information from the Caleb Doe scenario, instead this time lower the interest by one point to 4%. How much of a difference in interest do you notice? Keep in mind, the interest rate matters. The lower the better.

Is it possible to consolidate? If so, be careful. Sometimes you may have multiple loans from several sources. If this is the case, you may explore if consolidating is an option. Consolidating is when you combine several loans under one lender, and then work toward paying off the balance. Explore what consolidation loans may be available to you. **However, be careful!** You may not want to combine private and federal loans because you may lose any benefits that come along with the federal loans. Also, consider whether the interest rate for the consolidation loan would be lower than your current rate. The interest rate matters in your decision making. The lower the better.

Is it possible to use the snowball strategy? This strategy consists of paying off the lowest balance first. Why? This strategy will enable you to free up your monies the quickest by applying additional funds to your smallest debt first (while also paying the minimum payment on other debts). Once the smallest balance is paid off, then the monies can be used to make a larger payment on the next balance. This is also motivation! Each balance you pay off is motivating and inspires you to pay off the next one. It allows you to see that You Can Do It! Just know, the more you pay on the principal, the quicker you can pay it off without high accumulation of interest.

Remember, when you pay extra on a loan, make sure to pay it on the "principal." The lower the principal, the lower the interest amount you will have to pay. For example, there are options to make extra payments, but ensure it is on principal only. If writing a check, be sure to write "principal only" on the check. If you need clarity about how to do this, contact your lender directly and ask how to make extra payments on the principal only. I cannot stress enough how important it is to make extra payments on the principal (the amount you originally borrowed). If you do not specify, the lending institution will apply the extra payment to the principal and interest.

Is it possible to use the avalanche strategy? This strategy consists of identifying which balance has the highest interest rate and will cost you the most money. This strategy will take longer, BUT you will save the most money by paying off the balance (e.g., student loan, credit card) with the highest interest rate first. Remember all that interest Caleb Doe had to pay? The goal with this strategy is to avoid that. Remember, make extra payments on the principal, this will result in less interest in the long run.

Task: Are there one or more strategies you would prefer using? Describe which ones you would like to use below.

Create a budget. Another key strategy and great starting point for paying off your debt is budgeting. A budget is a spending plan that helps you to live within your means by tracking your spending habits. In other words, to spend less than you earn each month. Realizing where your money is going can be very helpful in promoting financial wellness. This can certainly be challenging as many people are drawn into excessive spending due to access to credit cards, loans, or even using money from their emergency fund! Credit cards and loans create an illusion that you have more money – yet remember you are only contracting with an entity to use their money and you must abide by the contract to pay it back, and there may be interest. We now know, due to the Caleb Doe exercise, that we want to avoid interest. So, let's create a budget to organize spending.

Budgeting is a basic financial planning skill. Question - **Have You Ever Played a Board Game?** What does it take to play a board game? Here are a few skills below:

- o First, you would most likely develop a strategy to avoid losing the game.

- o Second, to avoid losing, you must think ahead. In other words, what decisions would you make to strengthen your chances for making it to the end of the game and winning?
- o Third, you would probably look at everything you have, all your game pieces and options, then make decisions about how you could best use them to your advantage.

To win the game, you would need to plan. **Let's have a little fun and engage in a Basic Financial Planning – Challenge!** Starting right now, I challenge you to track your spending for 7 days. You can start now by taking out a piece of paper, your laptop, cell phone, or whatever may be convenient for you and writing down what you have spent so far today, if anything.

Example: Wednesday, January 10th

Cook Out Restaurant (spicy chicken meal)	$3.99 (Cash)
Amazon (outfit I couldn't resist)	$75.38 (Credit Card)
Subway (turkey sub meal)	$12.99 (Credit Card)
Total	$92.36

WARNING: Tracking spending is where many people get discouraged, bored, feel confined, or lose interest in the budgeting process. The task of writing down every way you spend your money may be daunting. However, I encourage you to hang in there! This challenge is only for 7 days, and the results can be eye-opening. Remember, you can keep receipts and engage in online ways to keep track. If you use credit or debit cards, the information is noted for you on your account site. There are many ways to make this process easier. Just remember, if you are using cash, ask for a receipt that you can place in a notebook, folder, box, etc. so you may document your spending over the 7 days.

After you have engaged in this Basic Financial Planning - Challenge for seven days, use the space below to write what you notice in **your spending** pattern.

Mark, highlight, or list the items that were necessary. Then mark, highlight, or list the items that were simply wants. What do you notice about your necessities versus wants?

Reflecting on the above questions and your 7 days of tracking your spending habits, are there any immediate ideas of what you would like to do differently? Are there certain habits you would like to change?

You did it! Now that you have tracked your spending and have an idea of your spending patterns, **on day 8, create a budget.** What is the purpose?

1. To create a plan based on the information about your spending habits, income, bills, etc.

2. To create a savings and emergency fund vision.

3. To have control over your finances for the long term.

Those are just a few reasons to create a budget. In my opinion, a great advantage is that a budget helps to promote a peace of mind, a sense of control, as well as empowerment over your financial situation. Let's keep budgeting simple by recognizing it is a plan or strategy for where your money will go. This is a way to be empowered and have a sense of control over your finances. There are several ways a budget can be created. For example, a traditional way is identifying your income, then each expense as well as the money allocated for each monthly. A traditional budget looks like the following:

Month and Year _____

Income	Monthly Total
Paycheck (after taxes)	$
Other Income (e.g., selling items)	$
Total Monthly Income	$

My Expenses for this Month

Expenses	Month Total
Rent or Mortgage	$
Insurance (renter's, homeowner's, car)	$
Utilities (e.g., electricity, water)	$
Internet, phone, cable	$
Groceries	$
Eating out	$
Medicine	$
Clothing, shoes	$
Childcare	$
School fees (loans, supplies)	$
Amount placed into savings account	$
Donations	$
Total Monthly Expenses	$

Income $ _____ - (minus) **Expenses** $_____ = (equals) _____

A little tip - There are certain expenses that may not occur every month, such as car insurance. I tend to divide that number by 12 and write that amount into the budget. That way, I am sure to have that money set aside by the time the bill arrives. It is a relief to know that specific money is sitting in my account and available when the time comes!

This is just a brief example of a budget. Be sure to add your unique expenses to the Expense column as only examples are provided above. Also, note your various sources of income, which may include child support or alimony. Once you integrate all your information, subtract your total expenses from your income. After doing this, you may find that your income exceeds your expenses. In this case, that is wonderful! Be sure to place a portion of your income into your savings or make an additional payment to your debt principal.

On the other hand, your expenses may exceed your income. In this case, review your budget and determine where you may cut or decrease certain expenses. For example, is there an internet plan with a lower fee? Is there a lower car insurance option? Take time to explore what types of changes you can make to your expenses. The goal is for your income to exceed (be higher than) your expenses.

30-Day Budget Challenge! – Develop and follow your budget for the next 30 days.

Task: Conduct an internet search for examples of budget sheets. Locate a free one that you can use, create your own, or visit the budget sheets at the end of this book. Overall, select one that works for you! After doing so, use the space on the next page to write about your experiences, successes, and challenges about building your budget.

Task: Does your income exceed your expenses or do your expenses exceed your income?

Task: After creating and reviewing your budget, what types of changes would you like to make to the budget, if any?

Task: Do you feel you could create a budget each month to help build your financial wellness? If not, what are the reasons why?

Task: What types of support do you need to stay consistent with budgeting? What is at least one step you can take to proactively engage with those supports?

5

THE ART OF THE SIDE HUSTLE

Self-expression, growth, and active investment – strategize your side hustle.

Let's talk about the art of the side hustle to build additional income streams. A key point is that having a side hustle does not equate to working more or adding "busyness" to your schedule. Remember, the theme of this book is financial wellness, therefore engaging in methods that promote a sense of empowerment versus overwhelm. Keep this framework in mind as we discuss side hustles.

A 2019 article titled, About 13M U.S. Workers Have More Than One Job, posted by the United States Census Bureau shares how many maintain full and part-time jobs with most being within the social service, health, and education sectors. It is interesting how these are within helping professions and whether maintaining multiple jobs correlates to the lower salaries often received by helping professionals. Throughout my career, I have engaged in multiple side hustles including weekend employment, evening employment, contracting with group practices, making beaded jewelry, decorating weddings and other events, authoring books, and more. Each of my side hustles has been enjoyable and are either in alignment with my social work skills or are an expression of my artistic side.

Your Side Hustle

Many may think the "side hustle" expression is new; however, this began decades ago. I recently watched a movie from the 1970's, and that was one of the expressions. You may also be familiar with the other expressions "gig" or "side gig." In other words, this terminology has been around for quite some time and just like everything else I have seen in my lifetime, comes back!

You may have multiple intentions behind engaging in a side hustle. I noted a few of mine above and the majority were for artistic expression and enjoyment as well as to enhance my skills. My primary aim for several side hustles was for enjoyment, and certainly additional income was an extra benefit. That is primarily what I hope your side hustle feels like - self-expression, growth, an active investment in your interests – then, for the income to be an additional benefit.

However, you may also engage in a side hustle out of need, to supplement your household income, pay medical bills, or even care for a loved one. You may also become interested in pursuing a side hustle as an entrepreneurial endeavor. Whatever the reason, when considering a side hustle or gig, ask yourself the following questions. Please note, you do not have to answer these questions right away. Take some time to ponder, then return to the questions when ready.

In what ways could a side hustle enhance your life? What are the reasons you would begin a side hustle?

What do you envision as a successful side hustle?

What are your intentions for the side hustle? In other words, what would you like the outcome to be? How much income would you like to make per week, month, or year?

What specific talents or skills do you want to use?

What are your life priorities (e.g., family, spirituality) and how will your side hustle fit into this?

Is the side hustle in alignment with your interests and values?

How will you work the side hustle into your current schedule?

What level of control or authority will you have over the side hustle (e.g., time contribution, location, freedom of creativity)? Will the side hustle allow you flexibility?

Who do you want to provide a service or product to (e.g., target population) and what need, want, desire, or problem are you seeking to address for that population?

What methods will you engage in to learn about your target population? What are their interests?

What marketing efforts will you use to target those interests? In what ways will you deliver your product or service? Will your side hustle be virtual or have a physical location?

What steps will you take to get your name out there, be recognizable, or build your reputation? What trust building activities will you engage in to encourage people to use your service or product?

Use What You Have

Everything matters! Use your experience for your side hustle. For example, have you attended recent trainings and enhanced your knowledge? Could you take the skills or information you learned from the training and integrate it into a side hustle? How can you take what you have and transition it into some type of business, whether for-profit or non-profit? In what ways can you leverage your knowledge, skills, and talents? Could you train others, consult, write books, or develop products? There is so much you can do!

Eventually, you may want to consider if your side hustle will just be something you do periodically, part-time, or if you would like it to be your full-time business. After you get a little more settled into your side hustle, you may be able to make that determination, or you may have your mind made up now that you want it to be a full-time business and design it as such. Remember, you can deliver your social work skills and personal talents in a plethora of ways, feel welcome to be creatively you!

A tip is to see what free training or courses you can access online or within your community for business development. For example, in North Carolina, the community colleges have what are called Small Business Centers. These centers provide free, short courses on topics including starting business, applying for grants, and even marketing strategies. Take time to invest in yourself and explore your community resources such as community colleges, financial institutions, and more for growth opportunities.

Task: Conduct an internet search to locate a Small Business Center at a community college in North Carolina. Review the listing of courses (please note, only North Carolina residents can register for the courses). Now that you have an idea of what free community resources may look like, conduct an internet search within your own state or geographic location. What services might your area community colleges, financial institutions, etc. provide? Describe your findings below.

Side Hustle Considerations

Consider how you will manage your time. Just as with any other form of employment or activity, you would want to give your 100%. What organizing strategies would you need to put into place to manage the side hustle, other employment, family, education, etc.? What type of support system will you have in place so you can manage the various dimensions of your life?

Another consideration is taxes. I am not a tax professional so I will stay in my lane (or within my areas of competency) and recommend that you study taxes in relation to your side hustle. For example, what are the reporting requirements to the Internal Revenue Service (IRS), how much should you save so you will be able to pay those taxes. Remember, at your full-time or certain part-time places of employment, they may withhold the tax amount for you. However, if you are an entrepreneur, you would need to figure these numbers on your own or through the support of a financial professional. Now that you have been provided a few tips about side hustles, let's explore ways to enhance your marketability to strengthen your financial wellness.

6

ENHANCE YOUR MARKETABILITY

Recognize your professional worth – then you will have confidence in knowing that you add unique value to the workspace.

Sydney Hart is a social worker who has developed the Hart Social Work Career Inventory. Hart found that there was a lack of information for social work students pertaining to career options and limited information about the diversity of roles one could fill as a social worker. As a result, the inventory was designed to enhance your awareness about various social work employment opportunities that may be in alignment with your interests. When pursuing financial wellness, it is critical to know your career options, to be open to growth and beneficial risks in career decision making, as well as traditional and non-traditional social work roles. At the time of this writing, the Hart Social Work Career Inventory was in the process of being evaluated through research methods and strengthened prior to use by the public. Hopefully, it will be available soon. In the meantime, let's talk about ways to enhance your marketability and income.

Build Your Knowledge and Skills. Enhancing your knowledge and skills through interdisciplinary opportunities is a strength. I have often said, *if there was a dual social work and business and/or law degree when I was in school, I would have taken that degree program.* To my knowledge, during the 1990's, there was not a specific program in my geographic location. However, there are many options now of ways to obtain a dual degree within your areas of interest and enhance your marketability. I appreciate how social work programs are now adjusting to the career landscape and the skills that employers are seeking across work environments. For example, there are now dual degree graduate (including masters and doctorate combinations) programs in social work and:

- Business Administration
- Divinity
- Public Health
- Juris Doctor
- Law and Legal Studies
- Bioethics
- City Planning
- Fine Art
- And the list goes on!

However, if you have already attained your masters or doctorate degree, there are still options to enhance your knowledge in other areas of interest. For example, there are certificate programs. These are brief (e.g., a few months) and specialized in a certain area. Several years ago, I completed a certificate program to become a certified trauma professional. Although well-equipped through my degrees, I wanted to stay current in knowledge about trauma and new interventions. However, certifications generally expire, but you will still have your knowledge. **Note**: The certifications cost, so plan this as part of your budget.

Another alternative is webinars, conferences, and symposiums in your areas of interest. There are multiple organizations that post upcoming events on their websites. Furthermore, I created a brief video on my YouTube page (Dr. Veronica Hardy) called, How to Build Business Savvy: Crafting Your Social Work Degree. In other words, there is an abundance of information online that can contribute to your professional and personal growth. In addition to the use of career inventories, exploring dual degree options, and engaging in additional training, defining your skills is also a way to enhance your marketability.

Define Your Skills. Another way to enhance your marketability, whether seeking or building side hustles, or even pursuing full-time employment is to clearly define your skills. What does this mean? Not too long ago, I wrote an article for The New Social Worker: The Social Work Careers Magazine titled, Transitioning from Graduation to the Workforce: Entering the New Landscape. In other words, taking the time to realize the value of your class assignments and the types of skills that result from class activities. Oftentimes, the skills you developed during your education may be overlooked – by you! Don't overlook your skills. Acknowledge and document them. How would you go about doing that? Here are a few tips.

Break down what the skill means. In other words, what skills make up a particular skill? For example, one of my skills is writing but what does this really mean? What skills go into the writing I do? Here are a few:

1. Information gathering
2. Idea development
3. Time management
4. Editing
5. Marketing

How might these terms translate into me explaining my skill of writing to an employer hiring for an Employee Relations Consultant? Here is an example of what I might say:

"I am currently an author of multiple publications with a strong writing skillset including information gathering, idea development, time management, editing, and marketing to diverse audiences. I am sure these skills are a great match for an Employee Relations Consultant due to the critical importance of the written form of communication for this position, the need to write in an inclusive and diversity-responsive manner, and the ability to meet agency timelines for written product development such as handbooks, announcements, and professional growth courses."

Do you see what I did? I took the broad skill of writing, clearly defined what this consists of, then showed how those skills could translate to a specific job position. Now, I invite you to give it a try. In the box below, list 3-5 of your skills.

Next, select at least one of the skills you have written above and list the "skills" that make up that skill. For example, remember my skill was "writing." The skills that make up the writing skill include information gathering, idea development, time management, editing, and marketing.

Conduct an internet search for a job that you may be interested in, for example, policy advocate, program manager, diversity and inclusion specialist, grant writer, researcher. There are so many options, seek out one that may be of interest to you for the purposes of this activity. After you have found a job and the position description, write below how your skills translate to the certain of the skills required for that position.

Review the example I have written above showing how I would translate my writing skills to the Employee Relations Consultant position.

This is good practice and very helpful in recognizing your skills and the various ways you can add value in diverse workspaces. Once you realize and define your skills, you will be able to market or promote them. **Side note:** This is also helpful in preparing for an interview! Another factor that can enhance your marketability is having a growth mindset.

Growth Mindset. You may recall that I mentioned growth mindset in an earlier chapter. Well, let's apply that same idea toward enhancing your marketability. Part of a growth mindset is debunking the myth that social workers do not make money. Yes, many social workers make over 6-figure incomes ($100,000+). It may be challenging to understand this because all you may have been exposed to in conversations or writings about social work salaries have been low incomes. However, many of the conversations or writings do not communicate the diversity of roles social workers fill and the amount of compensation.

In addition, there is a myth that all social workers only fill roles where "Social Worker" is the title. Certainly not! You are a social worker by your degree but that may not be your workplace title. For example, in my workplace, my title is "Professor." In other words, I am a social worker who fills the role of professor. There are many social workers with the title of "CEO" or chief executive officer, others are communications specialists, senators, entrepreneurs, university deans, and more! Build a growth mindset and shatter the myths. Social work skills can transition to many workplace settings. Throw away the myths and be open to a world of opportunities!

Learn the Art of Negotiation. Knowing your professional worth, skills, and value of your education enhances your marketability and opportunity to negotiate for higher income. The first tip was to "not" take the first offer. He informed me there is a range – low, middle, high – as far as salary. Many places make the first offer at the low range and leave themselves room to negotiate. As a result, it was important for me to be familiar with what the salary ranges generally were for the type of position I was applying for.

What did my professor encourage me to do next? The position I was applying for was with the "State." In other words, it was a State-funded position. He let me know that all State-funded salaries were made available to the public. So, I did an internet search, pulled up the job title and began to look at the various salaries. This knowledge gave me a great idea of the salary range for the position and how to negotiate.

Certainly, not all positions are state-funded, others note their concrete salary along with the position description, and others may say "negotiable" or "salary commensurate with experience" or avoid posting any information about salary at all. However, you can still conduct an internet search for positions like those you may be interested in, within that specific geographic location, and begin to study the various salary possibilities.

Earlier in this chapter, you took steps to define your skills. Having knowledge and confidence about your skills is critical during negotiation. Remember, some postings say "salary commensurate with experience" … therefore, you need to be able to explain your skills and experience with confidence. Also, be able to compare your skills and experience with that noted in the job description. Now, let's get ready to negotiate!

Scenario: Imagine you are applying for a Director of Diversity and Inclusion position at a local organization. The employer has offered a salary of $67,500 for the position. Since you have done your research about leadership positions focusing on diversity and inclusion, you may realize that could be quite low for your training and skills and the position responsibilities. Remember, generally employers are ready to negotiate based on the entity (e.g., sometimes positions are grant-funded and there may not be room for negotiation).

Task: Before we move forward, engage in the following. Conduct an internet search for leadership positions (e.g., Director, Specialist, Strategist) for diversity and inclusion. Explore the position descriptions and salaries. Discuss what you find.

Remember, this is just for practice purposes and a task to help you learn how to negotiate. Imagine that you qualified for the position and your skills and experience should be at the mid-range of the salary options (imagine that $67,500 was at the low range). What would you say to the employer when they call you back to hear your decision about whether you will accept the position? What words would you use to negotiate for a higher salary?

I remember when I entered negotiation discussions, I felt very uncomfortable. However, I still said what I had planned. It was like the following:

> "I am very excited about this position and enjoyed visiting the location and meeting the employees. I also appreciate that you feel I will bring value and that you have offered me this position. At the same time, I am wondering if the salary is negotiable based on my skills and experience and whether a salary of $75,000 would be possible?"
>
> The employer's response, "The salary is pretty firm, and it is a good match for your skills and experience."
>
> My response, "Thank you, but is there the possibility that it could be discussed further with the search committee prior to me making my decision?"
>
> The employer's response, "I will look into it and get back to you soon."

Generally, when the employer said that the salary was firm, I felt a little anxious and was about to give in, fearing I would lose the job opportunity. Here I say, make the decision that is best for you. I decided to stand my ground because I also had another job offer. Overall, determine what level of risk you are willing to take to negotiate, your personal and family needs, and whether you have a strong interest in the position. Ever since that experience, I feel comfortable negotiating. By the way, I did receive a salary higher than the employer's initial offer!

Negotiating your salary **should not stop** when you receive your position. For example, I had been at a job for several years and decided to explore what my peers were earning as well as the new hires I had been training. Do you know what I found? The new hires were being paid more than people who had been there for several years and who were carrying a much heavier workload!!! As a result, I contacted the necessary person, expressed what I found, and made my request for a higher salary. The person said, "That is nothing but the stroke of a pen." Next thing I knew, my salary was raised by several thousand dollars! Pay equity is critical as well as pay commensurate with your experience and workload. If you feel comfortable and safe doing so, advocate for yourself in the workplace.

Consider Fellowship Opportunities. Fellowships may come in various forms but are primarily short-term skill building opportunities where you also receive compensation or funding. This helps to enhance your marketability because you are immersed in a specialized area, possibly exposed to experts, and building new skills and knowledge. Some examples of fellowships are those offered through the Z. Smith Reynolds Foundation, Shared Hope International, Society for Research in Child Development, or the National Association of Social Work Foundation. These are just a few and there are hundreds more! Take time to learn more about fellowships by conducting an internet search, contacting your advisor within your degree program, or engaging with a mentor.

The Benefits of Building Mentorship Networks. The current career landscape is competitive and requires social work professionals with diverse skills, knowledge, experience, and confidence to respond to contemporary challenges. Engaging in mentorship allows support and structured guidance to strengthen academic performance, build support networks, and pursue employment. However, what is a mentor?

A mentor has qualities like that of a colleague and friend, provides advice and guidance about career goals. A mentor is a support to someone who is seeking professional growth and development – even growth pertaining to your finances. On the other hand, mentorship is not mental health counseling, clinical supervision, or academic tutoring. Consider the following questions:

- Have you put off your academic or career goals due to feelings of inadequacy?
- Have you ever questioned your knowledge, skills, and abilities as a student or social worker?
- Have you ever kept silent and felt "small" in a room where others seemed "big" although you had a great idea that was worth sharing?

If you have experienced the above, you are not alone. I have too. At times, I have allowed self-doubt to keep me still when I should have given myself permission to propel forward. At other times, I simply lacked the "know-how" and just needed someone to provide guidance and support. These feelings and experiences are real for many and effects job performance, career options, or even income.

Self-doubt is hindering and limits us in our choices and keeps us from taking exciting and prosperous career risks (e.g., just like when I packed up and moved across the country or when I paid off all my debt, resigned from my full-time job, and became an entrepreneur). There is great value in professional mentorship. I may never have been able to make such career leaps without my spiritual faith and people encouraging me through mentorship. Mentorship can help to cast out and throw away limiting beliefs such as self-doubt and imposter syndrome. Remember, you are NOT an imposter!!! You are trained and skilled, take time to honor and value your accomplishments and say Good-Bye to imposter syndrome!

One example of mentorship is through an effort I developed called, The Nelson-Hardy Mentorship Project (NHMP) for Social Workers, where more information can be found at www.veronicahardy.com. This effort is designed to promote social belonging by confronting vulnerabilities and feelings of imposter syndrome that hinder achievement of academic and career-related intentions. Certainly, this is only one example of a mentorship effort. There are many others that are nation-wide and may meet your academic and career needs. Also, please visit one of my featured articles in The New Social Worker Magazine titled, 3 Tips for Selecting the Right Social Work Mentor for You. It is important to be intentional in choosing a mentor who is in alignment with your career and/or financial plans.

Task: Conduct an internet search for mentorship programs for college students. Try keywords such as mentoring, students, college, high school, first-generation, low income, career. After you locate mentoring programs, describe what you find below. For example, what is the program's purpose? What population does it target (e.g., age, race, economic status, career type)? Describe if you located a mentorship program that may be beneficial for you.

Overall, consider the importance of your skills, talents, and values when seeking to enhance your marketability. Make determinations about how you can both invest in and understand yourself.

7

LET'S MAKE THIS REAL

Move from thought to reality – lay the foundation, then build upon it.

We are social workers, so before we go, we must make this real by putting some intentions in place. Action is critical when it comes to financial wellness. You have already taken action by completing the tasks throughout this book to build your financial wellness. Now, it is time to create your own unique plan. Be a change agent in your own financial life!

In the beginning of this book, I mentioned how there is no secret to paying off debt. Generally, people know the basics such as making a budget, building an emergency fund, donating, and living within their income. However, although this "seems to be simple" why is it such as challenge? Generally, it is the thoughts and emotions that make it a challenging process. What are the types of messages (also known as self-talk or even limiting beliefs) that may hinder our abilities to fulfill financially healthy tasks? Here are a few common messages: *I should be able to spend whatever I want; I have credit cards. Right now, my parents are paying for everything, so I don't need to save my own money. It will be too hard to stick to a budget. I can worry about debt when I graduate, right now it's all about fun. My money is tight, I don't have enough to save. I have always struggled with money and that will never change. I don't like thinking about money, it stresses me out.* Have you ever found yourself thinking these types of thoughts?

You may have noticed that there have been multiple questions about your thoughts and feelings toward finances throughout the book. This is because financial wellness has a lot to do with your mind. I invite you to use the space below to share your thoughts in response to the following questions.

What types of feelings or experiences underlie your thoughts toward finances? Is there fear involved? What would it take to move beyond your comfort zone so you can begin to live a financially healthy life?

Examining your thoughts, emotions, strategizing, and taking action are critical for staying on track toward financial wellness. Let's begin to confront the above concerns, apprehensions, doubts, or fears by engaging in the following steps:

Step 1: Identify Your Intentions

Have you ever aimed for a target and missed? That often happens with rigid goal setting. At times, a goal may be grand leading to overwhelm. In other words, it is too big and may lead you to give up before you even get started. Let's avoid this barrier by using a different approach. Instead, I like to use the word – intention. In doing so, consider your intention as helping to establish a sense of clarity and direction, not as an endpoint. There are many ways to reach a destination. Be flexible, be ready for adjustments, and view your intentions as steppingstones or new habits you would like to develop so you can move forward toward financial wellness.

In addition, make sure your new habits are in alignment with your values and interests. Have you ever made plans that were out of alignment with "you?" In other words, you are pursuing a certain intention because someone else said you "should" do it. I noticed whenever I have allowed myself to be pulled away from my own intentions, values, and interests, I experienced many internal red flags. Those red flags included confusion, struggle, frustration, questioning "why" did I choose this, and more! Remember, your life, your intentions. Avoid trying to fulfill someone else's beliefs about what you "should" do. Below, let's practice writing your intentions.

Task: Write at least one intention you would like to use as a steppingstone toward financial wellness. The intention can be big or small, short, or long-term. Be sure to make your intention specific and attainable. Then, to be clear on your steps and commitment toward your intention, also build objectives and action steps to help you navigate the journey. For example,

Intention: My intention is to implement the snowball strategy to pay off my smallest principal balance.

Objective: I will add $50 to the principal in addition to the monthly payment of my smallest loan.

Action Step: I will build and review my budget to determine where I can adjust my spending habits so I can have at least $50 to add toward the principal of my smallest loan.

Intention:

Objective:

Action Step:

Step 2: Identify Possible Challenges and Your Response

When developing an intention, it is good practice to identify possible challenges. In developing awareness of anticipated challenges, you can plan for them ahead of time. In other words, what challenges may arise when you are actively pursuing your intention and what will you do in response? For example,

Possible Challenge and Response: While pursuing my intention, I may experience the challenge of unexpected circumstances such as a medical expense, increase in gas prices, etc. In response, I will re-evaluate my budget to determine where changes can take place for me to still make additional payments on the loan principal. I may also have the option to develop a temporary side hustle or form of passive income to help supplement my income and continue to pursue my financial intentions.

Possible Challenge and Response:

Step 3: Evaluate Your Progress and Celebrate Your "Wins"

During this process, it will be important to implement ways to evaluate your progress through the following questions:

1. What is working?

2. Are you pleased with your progress?
3. What is not working?
4. What types of changes do you need to make to be successful and achieve the intention?
5. What have been your successes?
6. How can you celebrate your wins?
7. How does it feel to be successful with your intention?

Step 4: Evaluate Your Emotions and Ways of Thinking

As you pursue your financial wellness intention, continue to write your financial narrative. For example:

1. Describe your mindset.
2. Identify thoughts you have been experiencing throughout the process. Write about your successes.
3. Write about emotional reactions such as joy or stress.
4. Identify what triggered the emotions.
5. Discuss the effects of the emotions – did they motivate or discourage you?
6. Discuss ways you can continue moving forward toward your intentions even if experiencing discouraging emotions.
7. Describe what you have done in response to challenges.
8. Write about the ways you have coped with making financial changes. Identify your financial hopes.
9. Write about the changes you see in yourself – behaviors, thoughts, emotions.
10. Write about the ways you would still like to grow.
11. Describe actions you could take to pursue that growth.

Another Creative Way to Take Action

Maybe you would like a more creative and artistic way to pursue your intentions than the steps above. This method taps into your creative side and allows you to take small steps to help decrease fears, apprehensions, and stress about finances. This idea involves visualizing where you want to be with your financial health and wellness.

Visualization is a common technique used in social work practice and very much in alignment with a growth mindset. Visualization is when you take your mental idea of something and place it into a tangible form to make it real or attainable. For example, you may have heard of a vision board, vision journal, a hope or vision card, a letter to self, vision video, or even a vision screensaver. All these methods are designed to help you create your intentions, hopes, or goals through words, images, or other creative techniques.

In other words, you have a visual of what you would like to see manifest in your life. This visual helps to give shape and clarity to your thoughts and ideas. Have you ever considered creating a vision for your financial wellness? If not, why not give it a try?

Task: Begin learning about the various vision techniques by conducting an internet search. You could search for terms including vision board, dream board, vision journal, letter to self, etc. Then, discuss below your understanding of the purpose of these techniques.

Now, it is time to determine what method you are interested in. Would you like to video record a message to yourself about your vision? Would you like to create a screensaver for your cell phone or desktop with images and words that represent your vision? Would you like to write a letter to yourself about your vision or create a card? Do you have a journal where you can capture your thoughts about the vision? Do you have a big piece of paper or other material where you can make a vision board with images and words? There are so many methods even beyond what is mentioned here. Choose what may work best for you and describe below the reasons you are selecting that vision method.

Next, create your vision in your method of choice. Take as much time as you need to complete your visualization project to truly capture your financial wellness goals, intentions, and hopes. Remember, you can use just words, just images, recordings, or a mixture of many techniques. This may take a day, a week, or a couple weeks. Whatever your timeframe may be is fine to help refine your vision and intentions. Maybe on the first day, you can write your thoughts. Another day, you might collect images from newspapers, magazines, or online. The next day, you may explore colors that reflect your vision. There are so many ways to move toward completion of this project. Be sure to move at your pace, a little each day. Once you have developed your visualization project, describe what you have created.

Now that you have your visual, it is time to do something daily to create movement. Begin by imagining yourself moving forward toward the vision. What steps do you see yourself engaging in? What do you see yourself doing first? What did it take to get to that first step? Write what you are imagining below.

Remember how I previously mentioned how feelings and emotions also affect financial wellness? Recognizing your feelings and emotions are also an important part of this visualization process. As you imagine a step, allow yourself to notice the emotions that arise. We do this daily in other life experiences without even considering it. For example, when there may be a thunderstorm outside and you visualize yourself staying home from work. What emotions did you experience? Peace, relief, excitement.

Another example, when you are visualizing (hoping) receiving a raise, you may feel joy. These are just a few examples. Try visualizing your first step and allow yourself to experience the emotions that arise. If you have a challenging time describing your emotions, a tip is to conduct an internet search for a list of emotion words. This can be very helpful when seeking words beyond those in common use such as happy, angry, and sad. Describe your emotions below.

Focus on one step at a time. Imagine first, use your mind, then create. Remember, do not overwhelm yourself or make the steps too big and become discouraged. Visualize the specific steps every day as you move toward the vision. Make this a daily practice to help make your financial intentions a reality.

In Closing

Well, we have reached the end of this leg of your financial wellness journey. In other words, this book was just a starting point. It is time to consider what you will do next. What are your next steps in taking the reins of your financial wellness journey? For example, will you re-read this book? Will you implement some of the tasks and activities again to measure your growth and change? Will you visit and implement some of the creative financial practice ideas noted later in this book? Write below what your next step will be.

Certainly, since I am an educator, I always like for my students to reflect on their learning experiences. So, are you ready for your last task? Let's go! Use the following space to reflect on what you gained from reading Let's Talk About Finances.

Discuss the tasks and activities you completed. What did you gain from those experiences?

Also, don't stop with you! Create a new legacy and begin to teach your loved ones, friends, and fellow social workers about finances. What are ways you can start building a new financial legacy?

Well done on your initial start to financial wellness and empowerment. Consider ways to keep moving forward by visiting the Creative Financial Practice Ideas with a list of 36 ways to be imaginative in how you move forward in your financial journey.

Congratulations on your journey to financial wellness!

CREATIVE FINANCIAL PRACTICE IDEAS

Below are several creative ideas to decrease unnecessary spending, build healthy financial habits, and promote financial wellness.

1. Set financial goals for your savings, emergency fund, retirement, and leisure activities.
2. Make sure your savings are in accounts that can draw interest.
3. Start couponing and seeking discounts to reduce your costs when shopping.
4. Prepare your meals and eat at home.
5. Grow your own food.
6. Declutter and sell any items you no longer use. You could sell on sites such as Facebook, at a yard sale, or even a consignment shop. Whatever items in good condition you cannot sell, donate. This has the additional benefit of helping you organize your space.
7. Declutter so you are aware of what you own. This will help to decrease the chances of purchasing items you already own by mistake.
8. Decrease temptation by unsubscribing from stores and other marketing sites or emails.
9. Pause before you purchase. Take a day or so to think deeply before you make a major purchase. Determine if it is truly needed.
10. Comparison shop, the same item may be cheaper elsewhere.
11. Sign up for trusted rewards programs for places you shop often.
12. Negotiate your salary.
13. Protect your health. Remember, the primary reason for debt is health expenses.
14. Shop at thrift stores or purchase products from yard sales.

15. Engage in a clothing and item swap with peers if you have something you do not need, and your peers have items you want.
16. When grocery shopping, make a list and stick to it. Do not go beyond the list.
17. Do not buy things just because they are on sale, you might not ever use them.
18. Re-evaluate your memberships to locations such as fitness centers and determine if you still need them or if you can cancel.
19. Re-evaluate your subscriptions, such as television apps. Again, if you do not use or need it, consider cancelling.
20. Stop or decrease using your credit card. Use cash only. However, if you are in an area that experiences consistent cash shortages, this may not be feasible for you.
21. Reduce your insurance premiums by shopping for a lower premium with other reliable companies.
22. Reduce your utility bill by determining if you can cut down on use. For example, observe if you leave your computer plugged in all day or certain lights on that are not being used. Turn off lights not being used, unplug your computer if fully charged, etc.
23. Develop a budget so you can track your spending habits.
24. Spend less than you earn.
25. Every 3 months, add 1% extra to your savings from your income. For example, if your take home income (e.g., your paycheck) is $2500 per month. You would add an additional $25 to your savings or any other interest-bearing account you may have. This helps to ensure that your savings are increasing. As a result, you will have the usual amount you have been saving, for example, 10% of your income = $250. Now you are adding an additional 1% = $25, so your saving amount will increase to $275 per month. This is gradual growth.

26. Explore all your benefits and free perks through your workplace.
27. Invest but be sure to thoroughly study your options first.
28. Study information about finances at least twice a week to build your financial wisdom. This could be articles, videos, books, podcasts, or other methods.
29. Visit your bank or credit union to determine what types of "free" financial education services are available.
30. If available, take a "free" financial course or attend financial events at places including your university, community college, bank, or online.
31. Be sure to re-evaluate your financial plans at least once a year to determine what types of changes could be made.
32. Locate a Student Loan Repayment Calculator to help you plan to pay off those loans early.
33. Obtain a financial mentor, someone who is out of debt or almost out of debt to support you in your financial freedom journey.
34. Gain healthy and safe side hustles or ways to develop passive income.
35. Review a copy of your credit report every year to make sure the information is correct. This will help you make sure there are no errors or fraud. Remember there are at least 3 primary credit reporting agencies Experian, Equifax, Transunion, that each have different information or files about your credit. Check your report at each agency.
36. Plan for major purchases (e.g., house, car, vacation, education) and set savings goals to help pay for it.

Are there more creative ideas you can think of?

SAMPLE BUDGET AND SAVINGS PLAN SHEETS

MONTHLY BUDGET

MONTH OF

TOTAL INCOME **OTHER INCOME / SAVINGS**

EXPENSES ITEM	BUDGET	ACTUAL	DIFFERENCE	NOTES
MORTGAGE/RENT				
HOUSEHOLD MAINTENANCE				
TAXES				
INSURANCE				
ELECTRICITY				
WATER				
SEWAGE				
GAS				
PHONE				
TRASH				
CABLE				
CELL PHONE				
GROCERIES				
ENTERTAINMENT				
CHARITY/DONATIONS				
FUEL				
AUTO INSURANCE				
CAR PAYMENT				
CHILD CARE				
CREDIT CARDS/DEBT				
LOANS				
DINING OUT				
SPORTING EVENTS				
LIVE THEATER				
CONCERTS				
MOVIES				
TOTAL EXPENSES				

MONTHLY BUDGET

MONTH OF:

INCOME

Date	Source	Amount

SAVINGS

Date	Deposit	Paid Date	Balance

MONTHLY

Total Income	
Total Budget	
Total Savings	
Total Expenses	

Notes

DEBT

Date	Deposit	Paid Date	Balance

BILL

Bill	Amount	Due Date	Paid Date

Budget Planner

Month: _____

INCOME STREAMS

AFTER TAX	BUDGET	ACTUAL	DIFFERENCES
Income			
Side Hustles			
Business			
Others			

FIXED AND VARIABLE EXPENSES

EXPENSES	BUDGET	ACTUAL	DIFFERENCES

SAVINGS

	TOTAL SAVINGS
Total Income (After Tax)	
Total Fixed Expenses	
Total Variable Expenses	
Savings - Income + Expenses	

SAVINGS TRACKER

SAVING FOR _____ AMOUNT _____ DUE BY _____

DATE	WITHDRAWAL	DEPOSIT	BALANCE
		TOTAL SAVINGS	

Savings Goal

Goal

Savings

Deadline

Date	Amount

Reminder

Notes

RESOURCES

CHAPTER 1

1. The American Academy of Social Work and Social Welfare, 2016 Progress and Plans for the Grand Challenges: An Impact Report at Year 5 of the 10-Year Initiative.
2. National Association of Social Workers, 2021 Blueprint of Federal Social Policy Priorities: Recommendations to the Biden-Harris Administration and Congress.

CHAPTER 2

1. Bank of America, Better Money Habits: Millennial Report Winter 2020.
2. National Association of Social Workers, Membership Workforce Survey 2007 - In the Red: Social Workers and Educational Debt.
3. U.S. Department of Education – Net Price Calculator.
4. U.S. Department of Education, College Affordability and Transparency Center.
5. The Wall Street Journal, 2021, Nitashia Johnson, USC Pushed a $115,000 Online Degree. Graduates Got Low Salaries, Huge Debts.
6. U.S. Bureau of Labor Statistics Occupational Outlook Handbook – Social Work.

CHAPTER 3

1. NASW Issue: Support Loan Forgiveness for Social Work Students and Graduates 2015.

2. The New Social Worker: The Social Work Careers Magazine, www.socialworker.com.
3. Annual Credit Report, www.annualcreditreport.com.
4. U.S. Department of Education, www2.ed.gov/fund/grants-college.html.
5. Consumer Trade Commission, www.consumer.ftc.gov/articles/free-credit-reports.

CHAPTER 5

1. United States Census Bureau, 2019, Julia Beckhusen, About 13M U.S. Workers Have More Than One Job.

ABOUT THE AUTHOR

Dr. Veronica Hardy is a first-generation college grad and first African American female Professor (tenured) within her academic department. She has navigated her own experiences of self-doubt, imposter syndrome, and being "the only one," which have fueled her ambition to provide mentorship to students and fellow social workers. Dr. Hardy is currently a Professor of Social Work, a licensed clinical social worker, and author. She earned her Master of Social Work degree from West Chester University and doctorate in Counselor Education and Supervision from Regent University.

In honor of her family, she started the Nelson-Hardy Learning Institute, which houses several of her projects including Let's Talk About Finances, mentorship services for social workers, and online courses focusing on issues of daily living. She served as the mentor for the development of the HART Social Work Career Inventory, has served on doctoral dissertation committees, and proudly supports her students' endeavors as they flourish in their professional identities.

Dr. Hardy has fulfilled multiple roles including Vice Chair of the North Carolina Social Work Certification and Licensure Board, United Way of Robeson County Board Member, Board of Copy Editors for the International Journal of Social Work Values and Ethics, and professional consultant to Doing it for the Kingdom, an anti-human trafficking nonprofit. She has been proactive in serving her profession and community.

Throughout her career, she has provided services in settings including residential treatment facilities, maintained a private counseling practice, and served as a faculty member in social work and mental health counseling programs. Dr. Hardy has focused her attention on social justice issues including child sex trafficking, racial disparities, and inclusive teaching methods for persons with varying abilities.

Dr. Hardy has publications including A Letter to My Sisters: Reflecting on God's Promises, The Process of Grief: The Underrated Form of Self-Care, Becoming Un-Tangled: Eight Simple Strategies for Cleaning Up Your Life, Mind, and Habits, and Becoming Un-Tangled: Pray with Intention. She hosts the podcast, There is Power in Your Story, is a featured article writer and YouTube content creator for The New Social Worker Magazine, as well as the creator of The Social Work Lounge Facebook group for social workers. To learn more, visit www.drveronicahardy.com and www.veronicahardy.com.

THE UNDERRATED FORM OF SELF-CARE

THE PROCESS OF GRIEF

This workbook is designed to normalize the grieving process for helping professionals when coping with loss in the workplace.

BY DR. VERONICA HARDY
WWW.DRVERONICAHARDY.COM

Available on Amazon!

Dr. Veronica L. Hardy

Becoming *Un*-Tangled

8 Simple Strategies for Cleaning Up Your Life, Mind, and Habits

Available on Amazon

NOTES

NOTES

NOTES

NOTES

NOTES

Made in the USA
Middletown, DE
31 October 2023